TO BE
OR
NOT TO BE
An Admin

BONUS: EMBRACING AI AS AN ADMINISTRATIVE PROFESSIONAL

TEEKWA SCARBOROUGH

CITIOFBOOKS, INC.
3736 Eubank NE Suite A1
Albuquerque, NM 87111-3579
www.citiofbooks.com
Hotline: 1 (877) 389-2759
Fax: 1 (505) 930-7244

Ordering Information:
Quantity sales. Special discounts are available on quantity purchases by corporations, associations, and others. For details, contact the publisher at the address above.

Printed in the United States of America.

| ISBN-13: | Softcover | 978-1-963209-92-1 |
| | eBook | 978-1-963209-93-8 |

Library of Congress Control Number: 2024904481

Table of Contents

Introduction

Becoming an administrative assistant was not the career path I initially chose. I tried to steer clear of going down that path. It was my impression that being an administrative assistant meant being a slave to a master. I wanted to be a businesswoman who owned her own business, but I was unsure of what type of business I wanted to start. One thought was becoming an event planner. However, as life went on, my career path began to change due to circumstances in my life. I became a young single mother of twins, both of whom had medical issues. Then the unthinkable happened, and I had to painfully deal with the death of my first-born twin. Naturally, I put my dreams of owning a business on the back burner. I didn't have like-minded entrepreneurs around me at the time. Although I had a strong family support system, we were taught from a young age to finish high school, go to college, and get a good job. Owning a business was never discussed, but I knew I was destined for greater things; I just didn't know what it would be.

After starting college, I changed my major several times because I still wasn't sure what I wanted to do. I knew I didn't want to become a secretary, which is interchangeable today with administrative assistant. Running errands, fetching coffee, and sitting at a desk all day didn't sound exciting to me. But as much as I tried to avoid the role, it landed at my feet anyway. I had no experience as an administrative assistant, but in my first interview, my former boss saw something in me and gave me a chance.

I wasn't intimidated by the other assistants who had years of experience. I took my new position as a challenge. After being an assistant for one year, I had developed more technical skills than many of the other assistants. Most of them had been with the company since high school and were used to the old-school ways. That old-school approach meant more work for me, but I knew there was a more efficient way to get things done.

Starting the job with no experience, I took advantage of every free training class the company offered. I already had a great personality, was eager to learn new things, and had a desire to assist wherever needed. After completing numerous training courses, I wanted to apply what I had learned to my daily work. I created PowerPoint presentations from scratch, wrote reports, made spreadsheets, and even typed a dissertation for someone's Ph.D. When my department didn't have enough work for me, I reached out to my staff director to make myself available to assist other departments. You have to be a go-getter and take charge of your own professional development.

Working in any company offers a great opportunity, no matter the industry. I can work in any industry and be a great assistant. However, you must have a strong foundation as an assistant, which includes having strong technical skills, communication, organization, time management, and follow-up skills. These are necessary to meet the demands you'll face.

Being an assistant can be an underdog position in any industry or career, but it can open doors to your desired career path. At one point, I had to stop attending college because I wasn't sure what career path I wanted to pursue. I was changing my major almost every year, and it wasn't getting me anywhere. I needed to stop and really think about what I wanted to do. I knew I wanted to assist people but didn't think being an assistant was for me, as I didn't want to stay at my desk all day. One day, while on the train, I saw an ad for Monroe College listing different majors. The one that stood out to me was Information Technology (IT). A career in IT would still allow me to assist people, but it would also allow me to travel and not be confined to a desk. I visited the school, attended an orientation, and spoke to professors in the IT department. The field interested me, so I signed up for the next semester. Three years later, I graduated top of my class with a 4.0 GPA, Cum Laude!

I share this story to show that being an assistant can be a stepping stone to your desired career. I completed my internship with the company and continued working in the IT department while still holding my assistant position. So, why am I not in IT today? I applied for many positions, but some required certifications, or they wanted someone with 5-10 years of experience. While working in the IT department, I had a wonderful manager who pointed out my strengths. She praised my qualities as an assistant and how well I was appreciated by the employees I supported. We discussed my career goals, and she pointed out that my skills could lead to a promotion as a supervisor over the administrative team. So, I stayed where I was needed most and took my career as an assistant to the next level. Eventually, I was promoted to Administrative Supervisor.

Over the years, within our administrative community at the organization, several administrative assistants transitioned into roles of their choice after supporting their clients. One assistant became an examiner, while others moved into public relations, analytical roles, or business administration positions. This proves that being an assistant is a powerful career that can lead to opportunities in other fields. Don't underestimate it—assistants rock!

Chapter 1: Technical Skills

As an assistant, it's crucial to be ready to take on basic tasks. In every job, training is important, but knowing the basics upfront can significantly help your boss and allow you to handle things that don't require extensive training. For example, you may be asked to type a memo, draft a letter, or schedule meetings—essential tasks that lay the foundation for your work as an administrative professional.

When I began my journey as an administrative assistant, I didn't have any formal administrative skills. The only thing I knew how to do was type (thank God!). When I was hired, it wasn't because of my technical qualifications but because God blessed me with someone who took a chance on me. I was willing to learn, and I showed enthusiasm during the interview. Now, this doesn't happen for everyone, so I highly recommend familiarizing yourself with the basics of Microsoft Office (Word, Excel, PowerPoint, etc.). There are plenty of software tutorials available online, many of which are free. Microsoft itself offers classes, and YouTube is one of my favorite places to learn. It's important to find the right instructors— those who are energetic and straight to the point.

I taught myself many software programs because I am self-motivated and wanted to excel at my job. I spent time playing around with different tools until I felt comfortable using them to get my work done. At the organization where I worked, Microsoft Word, PowerPoint, and Excel were essential for drafting letters, reports, and creating presentations. It's imperative to be proficient with these tools! Fortunately, all software programs have help or tutorial features, often represented by a "?" in the toolbar, which provides step-by-step instructions when you're stuck or forget how to complete a task.

I remember when I was responsible for logistics during a large meeting and had to create letters manually, adding names and addresses one by one. A colleague showed me how to use the mail merge feature in Word, and it was like the gates of heaven opened. It made the process so much easier! Not knowing more efficient ways to complete tasks can make you feel frustrated and inefficient. But when you gain that technical experience, it empowers you and allows you to fully support the people who rely on you.

Over time, I realized I needed to continually build my technical skills to be effective and efficient. I attended classes to enhance my knowledge. Some colleagues didn't know how to help, or perhaps didn't want to share, but I made sure to learn what I needed to excel in my role. Being in this field, you must have the technical skills necessary to succeed. Over my 20 years as an assistant, I've mentored, trained, and supervised many others. This career has stretched me, but I've also stretched myself by seeking out opportunities to grow.

If you know you have what it takes to be an asset to your company or are thinking about becoming an assistant as a career move, I'm here to provide you with the necessary training and lifelong coaching to help you on this journey.

Remember, it's not just about mastering the software that belongs to a company—you will be trained on specific systems. But it's crucial that you have foundational knowledge to at least navigate the basics, such as turning on a computer!

Software Skills Needed and Business Software Applications Used by Administrative and Executive Assistants

What computer programs should an administrative assistant or executive assistant know? Here's a broad overview of the technology skills needed by administrative professionals, specifically relating to software applications.

Technology Includes Software and Hardware:

When we talk about "technology," we're referring not just to software, but also hardware like computers and office equipment such as telephones and copy machines. Administrative assistants need good-to-great technology skills because they use a variety of business software applications daily.

Scheduling, Calendars, and Email:

Administrative and executive assistants often manage schedules and calendars for their managers, executives, and entire departments. Microsoft Outlook is a popular choice for this, as it also doubles as an email application. Some admins use Google Docs (with Gmail) for scheduling and email, which is another strong alternative.

Desktop Publishing (e.g., Newsletters, Flyers, Invitations):

Administrative professionals who prepare newsletters, brochures, invitations, or other in-house publications often use desktop publishing software. Microsoft Publisher has been a popular choice for years. However, as of October 13, 2026, Microsoft Publisher will reach its end of life and no longer be included in Microsoft 365. Users will need to transition to other tools.

Fortunately, there are many alternatives, such as Canva, an online service for creating and distributing newsletters, flyers, and more. Canva offers user-friendly templates and real-time collaboration, making it a fantastic option for teams. Alternatively, you can use Microsoft Word to create newsletters and save them as PDFs, which can be distributed easily. The options for desktop publishing are vast, and the software landscape is continuously evolving.

Word Processing (e.g., General Correspondence, Reports):

Microsoft Word remains the go-to tool for creating correspondence, reports, and documents. Word is packed with features that make document formatting easier and more efficient, allowing you to produce polished materials quickly. Whether you're new to administration or a veteran, it's worth learning as much as you can about Word's capabilities. You'll discover features that can turn your basic document into something that looks like you spent hours on it—even if it only took 30 minutes!

Google Docs is another excellent alternative that offers similar capabilities, especially in collaborative settings. Open-source options like LibreOffice and OpenOffice are also available for free, offering word processing, spreadsheets, and more.

Spreadsheets (e.g., Project Tracking, Budgets, Inventory):

Excel is the top choice for managing spreadsheets. It's highly versatile, with features that range from simple data entry to advanced functions like formulas, pivot tables, and complex queries. While Excel may seem challenging to learn at first, it's worth the effort. Spreadsheets are widely used in office settings for tasks like project tracking, budgets, and inventory management. If you're considering or already in an administrative role, Excel is a tool you need to master.

Note-taking (Including Taking Minutes):

OneNote, another Microsoft product, is becoming increasingly essential for administrative professionals. It offers much more than basic notetaking, including audio recording, embedding content, and sharing notes publicly or within teams. You can download it for free if it's not already installed on your computer. Evernote is another popular option for notetaking with features like screen capture and organization tools.

Additionally, AI-powered platforms like Otter.ai are emerging, offering features such as real-time transcription, automatic summarization of meeting notes, and action item tracking. These tools can enhance productivity by ensuring that important details from meetings are accurately captured and easily accessible.

Database Management (Record-Keeping and Contacts Management):

Microsoft Access is a commonly used database management software, especially in businesses that use Microsoft Office. Access has both backend (for designing databases and reports) and frontend (for entering and updating data) capabilities. Many businesses also use Customer

Relationship Management (CRM) software like Salesforce, HubSpot, or Zoho CRM to manage customer interactions. As an administrative professional, you may work with CRM tools to enter data, run reports, or analyze customer interactions.

Slide Shows and Presentations:

Microsoft PowerPoint remains a staple for creating presentations. Whether it's for internal meetings or client-facing presentations, knowing how to create professional slides is a critical skill. Start by learning the basics of PowerPoint and master features like templates and slide transitions. Over time, you can advance to more complex features such as animations and multimedia integration.

So, let's recap the essential software and skills that administrative professionals should know:

- **Scheduling and Email:** Microsoft Outlook, Gmail, and Google Calendar.
- **Desktop Publishing:** Canva, Microsoft Publisher (until 2026), and Microsoft Word.
- **Word Processing:** Microsoft Word, Google Docs, LibreOffice, and OpenOffice.
- **Spreadsheets:** Microsoft Excel, Google Sheets.
- **Note-taking:** Microsoft OneNote, Evernote, Otter.ai.
- **Database Management and CRM:** Microsoft Access, Salesforce, HubSpot, Zoho CRM.
- **Slide Presentations:** Microsoft PowerPoint, SlideShare.

What Else?

There are many other tools and software you may encounter, depending on the industry and the specific needs of your organization. It's important to stay adaptable and continue learning as new technologies emerge.

Additional Tools to Explore:

- PDF Management: Adobe Acrobat is a must for creating and managing PDFs. It's especially useful for creating forms and handling document security.
- Graphics and Design: Adobe Photoshop Elements is a powerful tool for creating and editing images, even if you're not a professional designer.

These are just a few examples of the technical skills you'll need, but depending on your industry, there could be more to learn. Know your career path and the industries you want to work in, and continue building the skills that will support your professional growth. Being an assistant is a rewarding career, but it requires passion, dedication, and a willingness to constantly improve.

Ultimately, you are a valuable asset to any organization or small business owner, and they depend on you to help fulfill their mission and vision.

Chapter 2: Customer Service

You Are the First Line of Defense

First impressions are everything. They help build a positive reputation in your industry and set you apart from others. As an assistant, providing top-notch customer service is one of the most important skills you offer. Whether you're working for CEOs, VPs, or other professionals, they are your customers, and you must treat them as such. Your job is to serve both internal and external customers daily.

It doesn't matter if you work in a dentist's office, bank, police station, or as a virtual assistant for a coach—everything you do falls under customer service. Managing calendars, answering phones, overseeing social media, and handling day-to-day tasks are all forms of customer service. As an administrative professional, your role is to deliver consistent and high-quality service to your customers.

At my organization, we referred to the people we supported as "clients." Initially, I didn't fully understand this concept, but I later realized that my job was not just about completing tasks—it was about providing the best-in-class service to my client/customers. I thought doing my job well was enough, but it turned out there was more to it.

I remember getting a "meets standards" rating on my performance appraisal and feeling confused and disappointed. I was sure I had taken care of all my clients. In my one-on-one meeting, one of the officers I supported said that while I performed well, I didn't "show my face" enough. In other words, I didn't connect with people by making eye contact or being visible. At that time, I was extremely shy, which doesn't work well in this line of work.

As an assistant, your employer needs to trust that you can understand and follow directions. You'll work with a variety of personalities, and some clients require more attention than others. When I received that feedback, I was upset at first, but I took it as a challenge to improve. I began completing assignments ahead of deadlines, greeting everyone in the office instead of just sending emails, and even went as far as personally delivering the officer's newspaper every morning. I wasn't going to be labeled as someone who just "meets standards."

Tips for Exceptional Customer Service:

- Communicate with your boss regularly to ensure smooth workflow.
- Keep your skills up-to-date, especially with technology.
- Practice excellent phone etiquette, including how to transfer calls to devices like a android or iPhone.
- Set up a professional voicemail with clear instructions on who to contact in your absence.
- Meet and greet new hires, and ensure you know everyone on your team, including backup support.
- Let your clients know when an assignment is completed— sometimes just finishing the task isn't enough.
- Provide regular updates on current assignments, including estimated completion times.
- Continuously aim to improve customer service, whether that's through developing procedure manuals, improving communication, or managing inboxes more effectively.

Key Administrative Tasks Related to Customer Service:

- **Calendar Management:** Scheduling and coordinating appointments while checking for potential conflicts.
- **Travel Arrangements:** Booking air or train tickets, hotels, and transportation, and handling reimbursement upon return.
- **Correspondence:** Typing and distributing emails and letters on behalf of your boss.
- **Attendance:** Managing timecards or timesheets as required.

- **Office Tasks:** Filing, printing, photocopying, scanning, proofreading, and distributing documents.
- **Contacts:** Keeping all contact lists and organizational charts up-to-date.
- **Backup Services:** Providing administrative coverage for colleagues and their clients.

Essential Customer Service Skills for Administrative Assistants

As administrative assistants, we interact with people every day—whether over the phone, in person, or online.

Here are some essential customer service skills that will help you excel in your role:

- **Active Listening:** Build trust by showing that you understand the client's needs. Ask open-ended questions and paraphrase to confirm understanding.
- **Smile:** Believe it or not, people can "hear" your smile, even over the phone. A genuine smile makes you more approachable and suggests trustworthiness.
- **Know Your Audience:** Different types of clients require different approaches. Know their business, their preferences, and their background so you can tailor your service to meet their needs.
- **Handling Difficult Customers:** Be prepared to deal with challenging situations professionally and effectively.
- **Confidentiality:** Clients must trust that their business information will remain confidential. Don't share client details with friends or others who don't need to know.
- **Courtesy:** Simple phrases like "please" and "thank you" go a long way in making a lasting impression.
- **Empathy:** Understand the customer's perspective. When you show empathy, you're more likely to find a solution that works for both parties.
- **Follow-Up:** Always follow up to ensure problems are resolved and that the client is happy with the outcome.

From "Meets Standards" to Exceptional – Teekwa's appraisal

After I implemented these improvements, my performance appraisal went from "meets standards" to this:

"Teekwa's customer service skills are exceptional. She is always customer-focused and strives to meet the needs of everyone. She efficiently manages multiple tasks, all while prioritizing client needs. Teekwa acts courteously and professionally when interacting with clients, listens attentively, and resolves issues quickly and effectively. She consistently follows up to ensure high-quality service and problem resolution."

I wasn't playing around—I'm not a "meets standards" type of gal!

Here are some strategies to elevate your customer service game:

1. **Open Channels of Communication with Your Supervisor:** Maintain regular dialogue to align your efforts with organizational goals.
2. **Stay Current:** Continuously update your skills to remain relevant in a dynamic work environment.
3. **Master Phone Etiquette:** From proper techniques to managing transfers, hone your phone skills for seamless communication.
4. **Leverage Technology:** Actively utilize tools like modern communication platforms and apps to streamline your workflow.
5. **Personalize Interactions:** Take the time to meet and greet team members and new hires. Personal connections foster a supportive work environment.
6. **Provide Timely Updates:** Inform clients when assignments are completed, demonstrating your commitment to service excellence.
7. **Enhance Procedures:** Develop and maintain procedural manuals, including Standard Operating Procedures (SOPs), to ensure consistency and efficiency.
8. **Improve Communication:** Foster transparent and effective communication with clients to address challenges promptly.

9. **Streamline Email Management:** Optimize email efficiency by leveraging tools such as filters, labels, and folders to categorize and prioritize incoming messages. For example, use filters to automatically sort emails into folders based on sender or subject, and labels to mark important messages for quick reference.
10. **Invest in Skill Development:** Enhance your technical prowess in applications like Word, Excel, and PowerPoint to boost productivity.

Additional Services:

In addition to the above, you may also provide:

- **Meeting Coordination:** Arrange and facilitate meetings, including scheduling, preparing agendas, and coordinating logistics.
- **Event Planning:** Assist in planning and executing company events, from small meetings to large conferences or gatherings.
- **Procurement Support:** Aid in procurement processes by researching vendors, obtaining quotes, and processing purchase orders.
- **Record Management:** Maintain organized and efficient record-keeping systems for documents, files, and other important data.
- **Technology Support:** Provide basic technical support for office equipment, software applications, and communication tools.

By offering comprehensive customer service support across various functions, you contribute significantly to the overall efficiency and success of the organization. Your dedication to excellence and professionalism enhances the experience of both internal and external stakeholders.

Personal Growth and Recognition:

- Transform your performance from meeting standards to exceeding expectations through dedication and continuous improvement.
- Take pride in providing exceptional customer service, prioritizing client needs, and resolving issues promptly and effectively.

Chapter 3: Communication Skills

You must have excellent communication skills. Strong speaking and writing skills will give you the opportunity to speak on behalf of your client(s). Having exceptional communication skills will instill confidence in your client, allowing them to trust you to represent them in both written and verbal communications. Your job is to take on as much responsibility as possible so your client can focus on larger issues within the company. Therefore, getting to know your client well is crucial.

I learned the importance of communication skills the hard way. I never enjoyed writing when I was in school, and I definitely didn't enjoy math. So, what did I like?! LOL. I was a creative thinker and always approached things differently. I enjoyed helping people who needed assistance. I loved reading books, but it was always the same type—romance and drama. I was never interested in mystery or thrillers; I preferred to watch those in movies. Okay, let me get back on track. As I mentioned earlier, I was extremely shy, so I didn't talk much. My emails were not always the best, and sometimes they contained grammatical errors. Some errors were obvious to me, while others weren't. Because of this, my bosses were hesitant to let me send emails on their behalf. This issue was reflected in my performance appraisals for a couple of years, and I didn't like it because it prevented me from being promoted, even though I worked my tush off all year.

It is important for your boss to have an admin who can write and speak on their behalf. I had the opportunity to work with a VP who was very tough and dedicated to her work. She didn't just give feedback to my supervisor; she would correct my writing and personally call me into her office to ask if I was offended by her corrections. I told her I appreciated it because I would rather know what I was doing wrong than not know. From that point on, she gave me advice on what I needed to improve, particularly my use of past and present tense. My supervisor signed me up for grammar and writing courses, and my writing and grammar improved. It improved because I became more conscientious about my writing. I learned that when it comes to writing, I have to take my time. Reading your work several times before clicking 'send' is worth the effort. Additionally, asking a co-worker to review an email before sending it can be helpful.

While I can't say I'm the greatest writer, I did become more confident in sending emails on behalf of my boss. It's a great feeling to be trusted to handle all aspects of communication. Communication skills aren't just about writing; it's equally important to speak clearly and communicate effectively with your clients on a daily basis. Whether it's related to their calendar, customers, or even a co-worker issue, you must know how to address these matters in a professional manner.

Here are some communication tips for working with your client:

1. Addressing Calendar Issues:

- Find time on your client's calendar for a weekly 15-minute one-on-one checkpoint. I strongly suggest scheduling these early in the morning if your client is an early riser. This allows you to resolve any calendar conflicts or discuss other items. Make sure you have a list of all pending tasks or questions. You can get a lot done in 15 minutes, so make the most of it.

2. Monthly Check-In:

- Schedule a monthly meeting to check in and review how you're doing. Are you meeting your client's expectations? Is there anything they would like done differently? If their request doesn't work for you, explain why. Loosen up during this meeting, and chat about non-work topics such as the weekend or family. Everyone loves talking about their kids!

3. The Drive-By:

- Sometimes your client is too busy to meet with you, so I recommend doing a "drive-by." This is for those busy clients who barely have time to eat, let alone meet with you to resolve issues. You might catch them between meetings or when a meeting is canceled or ends early. This is your chance to drop by their office and say, "Hey, I just wanted to check in and see if you need anything." It's also a good time to ask for something you may need from them. Even though you might be a master at your craft, showing your face and checking in with your client is important—they appreciate it.

4. Stay in Contact:

- Always stay in contact with your client via email, text, or phone, depending on their preference. You need to stay informed of their every move so that if there are any emergencies, you know how to handle them and get in touch with them.

Additional Communication Tips:

Manage the Message:

- Always communicate with respect, keeping the needs of others in mind while staying calm.
  - Identify the type of information the person prefers. Do they want just the facts? Do they like anecdotes? Communicating in the other person's preferred style will make your words more effective.
  - Focus on the issue, not the person. No matter how upset you or they might be, addressing the issue rather than attacking the person is the only way to succeed.
  - If this person is a regular part of your work life, find out if they prefer emails, phone calls, or in-person communication. Even difficult people appreciate being asked how they prefer to communicate.

Communicate Across Cultures:

- Cultural and language barriers can break down communication faster than a pileup during rush hour—and cause just as much damage. To communicate well with people from other cultures, follow this advice:

- ○ Speak slowly, not loudly. Raising your voice rarely makes someone understand you better.
- ○ Assume nothing and be specific. You may know how things work, but not everyone does. Provide details that you take for granted.
- ○ Consider written communication instead. Email can be reread before responding, which increases comprehension. However, occasionally pick up the phone so your tone can be understood more easily.
- ○ Mind your manners. When all else fails, say thank you and apologize when needed.

Convey Complicated Ideas:

- Break information into smaller segments and list them by number to help set expectations and ensure your message is clear.

  For example:
  - ○ Here are four ways to contact me while I am attending the conference:
    1. Mobile
    2. Email
    3. Text
    4. Hotel number

Make Communication Personal:

- With the rise of email, it's easy to minimize face-to-face interactions. While it may feel more efficient to stay at your desk and communicate electronically or by phone, this has its downsides. Isolating yourself hinders your ability to be a truly effective communicator. Avoid overusing email and request regular face-to-face meetings with colleagues when possible.

Why Meet Face-to-Face?

- First, it's hard to gauge tone through email. Second, people like to make eye contact and read body language—it's human nature.

Face-to-face interactions lend themselves to clearer and stronger communication.

Convey Your Image:

- Non-verbal communication is very important. Do you know what your workplace attire says about you? Be mindful of your organization's dress code. Dress to impress and keep it professional. Look at the people you aspire to be like and dress accordingly. If your goal is to become the president of a Fortune 500 company, dress as if you already hold that position.

The Benefits of Better Communication:

Improving your communication skills can have significant benefits. Getting ahead might be as simple as communicating your ideas in ways that others are comfortable with. People who communicate well are often perceived as more responsible and effective, which usually leads to raises and promotions.

Teekwa's Appraisal:

"Teekwa's communication skills are above the standard and expectations for her salary grade. Teekwa is poised in her communication with her colleagues as well as the clients she supports. She processes the letters for the xxx team, ensuring necessary corrections are made and effectively communicating with clients both verbally and in writing to ensure the correct templates and processes are followed in the future.

After consulting with the xxx Management Team and administrators, Teekwa prepared a communication for the xxx Group, outlining how administrative responsibilities would be handled moving forward. The information was well received and appreciated by the clients. Teekwa also prepared a housekeeping communication, distributed to clients, to serve as reminders of small but necessary administrative tasks."

Chapter 4: Organizational Skills

A powerful assistant is always on-point and can immediately bring order to chaos. As an assistant, you need to know everything that happens in your client's world. Whether you're working for a speaker, coach, CEO, or any other professional, you must have a strong understanding of the business line and what your client provides to their consumers. Organizational skills play a major role in your position. You have to be aware of their current status, such as a particular project for a CEO or bookings for a coach or speaker. Everything needs to be at your fingertips to maintain order in your workspace.

For example: Growing up, I was never organized. My room was rarely clean, and when I needed to go out or find a piece of paperwork, it would take me forever. I'd get frustrated, and when you're frustrated, it's hard to think clearly, so you're even less likely to find what you need. It wasn't until I took my time and cleaned up that I'd finally locate what I was looking for.

Surprisingly, when I became an executive assistant, my desk was always immaculately organized. I was at the forefront of the organization, representing the firm, my client, and myself. You know what they say, "First impression is the last impression."

My client, who was a senior vice president, was not organized at all. Her office was always a mess. Every time I created meeting folders for her, I had to create duplicates because she'd either misplace them or claim she never received them. So, I had to come up with a system that worked for both of us. It was crucial that we stayed on the same page with this new system. I suggested leaving non-confidential materials on my desk for her to pick up at her convenience and keeping confidential materials on her desk, clearly labeled "Confidential Meeting Material." Any other documents she needed to review were labeled "Read Me" and placed on her desk. While it may sound simple, this system kept both of us organized and saved me from having to create extra meeting folders.

Your client's calendar is their Bible. You need to know it like the back of your hand. If your client comes to you at any time, you should know where their next meeting is, when it is, and have all the necessary materials prepared. Your organizational skills need to be sharp to ensure your client's overall success.

The Importance of Organizational Skills

The question isn't whether you can do your job without staying organized—it's how well you can do your job and how you can do it better. Administrative assistants with strong organizational skills are more productive, make better impressions on their bosses, and are more likely to receive promotions than those with sloppy, inefficient work habits. Instead of letting your career get derailed by careless habits, take the time to get organized, and in doing so, you'll get closer to reaching your full potential in the workplace.

Efficiency

Inefficiency causes you to waste time searching for files, documents, or digging through old emails to track down missing information. You waste even more time switching between devices to gather information from different places. However, if you're well-organized, you can save hours each week, significantly increase your productivity, and reduce your stress levels. This is especially helpful if you find yourself taking work home. By being organized, you may actually be able to finish your workday at a reasonable time while still meeting all your deadlines.

Better Work Quality

Being organized helps you avoid costly mistakes, such as overlooking information or missing appointments. Losing track of a memo from your boss can lead to time and money wasting errors. Forgetting to write down important information can result in having to restart a project from scratch. Consider how easy it is to double-book yourself or forget a meeting if you keep multiple calendars instead of consolidating them into one. Getting organized helps you avoid mistakes and allows you to do your job with fewer errors.

Good Impressions, Imagine these two scenarios: The president of your company and a key client walk past your desk, which looks like a disaster area. Now, imagine an executive stopping by unexpectedly and finding your workspace well-organized and tidy. Being organized can help you make a positive impression on your supervisors, clients, co-workers, and visitors. You'll earn respect on behalf of yourself and your company by maintaining professional-level organizational habits.

Future Opportunities, The good impressions you make when the boss walks by your desk aren't forgotten—especially if your organized work habits are part of your daily routine. Good organizational skills can demonstrate to your supervisors that you're responsible, serious about your job, and capable of handling larger tasks. When it's time for promotions, your name could be in the mix simply because you're attentive, efficient, and well-prepared.

Organizational skills are essential in any career, but assistants wear many hats and need to stay on top of every task. When you're organized, you can prioritize tasks by importance and efficiently and effectively complete your duties.

When your clients see your potential and trust that you're handling things correctly, you're on the right path to ensuring their needs are being met. It also opens doors for other opportunities or positions. One of the officers I supported once encouraged me to work on an exam at one of the banks with the examiners. It was a great experience, but ultimately, it wasn't something I wanted to pursue as a career.

Teekwa's Organization Skills Appraisal:

"Teekwa's organization skills exceed standards. She consistently makes suggestions and is trusted by her co-workers, clients, and supervisors. Her

supervisor has appreciated her quick turnaround on deliverables, such as coordinating and maintaining a list of all the xxx firm's official names, addresses, and phone numbers for the EVP office. In addition, Teekwa has taken the lead on training efforts for a temp, handling it with confidence and ease. We will actively seek her input on more ad-hoc projects as they arise, as she is familiar with the specific requirements of the business area."

Chapter 5: Professional Office Etiquette

In the introduction of this book, I mentioned how I always wanted to own my own business, and part of that dream included wearing nice suits, even though I'm more of a jeans-and-sneakers type of person. Growing up, I was a girly girl who valued comfort, but in the workplace, I wanted to embody the power and professionalism that comes with wearing a sharp suit. I used to imagine myself standing at a large window in a beautiful office, dressed in my best.

It's about dressing for the occasion. Just like we dress up for special events like church or weddings, we should dress appropriately for the workplace. Our attire should reflect the importance of the job and the role we aim for. Dressing well not only affects how others see you but also how you see yourself. For me, I dressed like I was ready for a promotion every day. My hair was styled, my outfits were professional, and I maintained a positive attitude. My supervisor noticed and often complimented me on how I presented myself, even jokingly suggesting I should be a supermodel because of my height.

While compliments on your appearance are nice, you want to be known not only for how you look but also for the quality of your work.

The Importance of Professional Presence

I've worked with colleagues who had issues with hygiene, didn't dress appropriately, or shared too much personal information at work. If I noticed, you can bet others did too. This is where office gossip often starts. I made a point to avoid gossip and maintain my reputation. When you associate with gossipers, even if you're not participating, people will assume you're part of it. I stayed friendly with everyone, but I also knew when to distance myself to protect my professional reputation.

As an administrative professional, you are a representative of the company. Your reputation precedes you, especially when you deal with clients and colleagues outside the organization. I often worked with other admins or directly with clients, both domestically and internationally. When I finally met them in person, I always made a point to introduce myself. The positive feedback I received from them reinforced that I was doing my job right. When your boss brags about you, you know you're representing the company well!

Professional Office Presence

Professional office presence is about conducting yourself with respect, courtesy, and professionalism at all times. It's not just about how you look—it's how you behave. The way you present yourself affects the atmosphere in the workplace and how your coworkers view you.

We all know the difference between right and wrong in the workplace, but sometimes we may not realize the small mistakes we're making when it comes to etiquette. By keeping these tips in mind, you'll create a more positive and professional presence that will benefit your career.

Phone Etiquette:

- Answer the phone with a smile; it can be heard in your voice.
- Answer quickly and avoid using speakerphone.
- Use professional language—no slang.
- Record a professional voicemail message.
- Avoid placing callers on hold for too long without informing them.
- Never eat or chew gum while on the phone.
- Take complete and clear messages.
- Don't answer the phone angrily.

Text Etiquette:

- Only send texts when it's urgent.
- If you need an immediate response, call instead of texting.
- Don't send bad news via text.
- Always use proper punctuation.

- Proofread before hitting send.
- Avoid typing in all caps.

Video Calls:

As a virtual assistant or in any remote work role, video calls are a professional space. Make sure you're ready:

- Keep your desk clean and camera positioned well.
- Ensure your background is neat and free of distractions.
- Dress professionally, at least from the waist up, even if working from home.

Your boss and colleagues rely on you to maintain professionalism, and part of that is how you present yourself. Whether it's in person, over the phone, or through technology, professional presence matters.

Use Common Sense:

- Think before you act.
- Don't assume; ask questions if you're unsure.
- Always follow through on your commitments.
- Finish what you start.
- Be proactive and come up with best practices to benefit the team.

If you support a coach, speaker, or entrepreneur:

- Listen actively.
- Speak clearly and answer all questions.
- Focus on the client and pay attention to detail.
- Be knowledgeable and willing to go the extra mile.

Keeping Calm Under Pressure

An assistant's ability to remain calm under pressure is crucial. When you can keep your cool, you set the tone for the office. Staying calm and collected shows that you are resourceful and prepared, and it helps create a more productive work environment. Always stay one step ahead and be ready for anything.

Communication Tips:

Good communication is essential for a productive workplace. Use polite language, say "please" and "thank you," and always listen carefully to others. Use your indoor voice and avoid interrupting your colleagues when they are speaking.

Body Language:

Show respect by giving your full attention to others. Make eye contact, face the person you're speaking with, and pay attention to your posture. When greeting someone, stand up and offer a handshake if appropriate.

Managing Emotions:

When you're upset or dealing with a difficult situation at work, take a moment to pause and process before responding. It's important to avoid speaking out of frustration or making provocative remarks. When receiving constructive feedback, listen and try not to become defensive. Use it as an opportunity to learn how others perceive you.

Avoid Taboo Topics:

Be careful about what you share at work. Avoid discussing personal matters like politics, religion, or salaries. Keep your personal life separate from your professional environment, and only discuss personnel matters with the appropriate individuals.

Time Management and Respect for Others:

Arriving at work early and staying late when necessary shows respect for your job and your colleagues. Be on time for meetings and complete your tasks promptly. Respect your coworkers' time by meeting deadlines and responding to messages in a timely manner.

By presenting yourself professionally, staying calm under pressure, and practicing good communication, you will build a strong professional presence that positively impacts the workplace.

In a Nutshell:

- Come to work well-rested and dressed appropriately.
- Don't be a distraction to others.
- Speak quietly and respect your colleagues' space.
- Clean up after yourself and respect others' property.
- Present yourself in a way that reflects well on both you and your company.

You should always remain professional at all times and maintain a positive attitude because people do notice. No matter how skilled you are, a negative attitude can leave a lasting impression that may harm your reputation. It can lead to poor performance reviews and could even stand in the way of promotions.

I knew an assistant who didn't have the best personality and was quick with sarcastic remarks to anyone who came to her desk. While she may have thought she was being playful, others were offended and hesitant to approach her. As a result, many clients avoided asking her for assistance. Be mindful of how you present yourself, both in words and actions. Body language is crucial when you're on the front line of your organization. If you're seen as unapproachable, that could greatly impact your ability to do your job effectively.

As an administrative professional, your body language should always convey, "How may I assist?" It's important to leave any personal issues or negative attitudes at the door. Strong interpersonal skills are essential in any role, but especially when you're an assistant.

Teekwa's appraisal:

"Teekwa's interpersonal skills exceed the standards. She is easy to work with and maintains a positive attitude. She is proactive in asking the team

about their needs to make their jobs easier. She collaborates well with her supervisor and is encouraged to continue in the positive direction. Teekwa has demonstrated the following: including her supervisor in email status of her projects, updating her on new business needs and requests that may arise especially when faced with critical situations. She volunteers when the need arises whether coming in to provide physical coverage and/or remote. Teekwa's ability to collaborate and train a temp within a short time frame has proven to be extremely helpful while she is away. She has good ideas to further build her relationship and collaboration skills and she is encouraged to move forward with them."

Chapter 6: Knowing Your Boss' Industry or Business

As an assistant supporting one or more team members with clients from various industries, it's essential to give each person the respect and attention they deserve. It's extremely important to understand the industry and business of each individual you support. To deliver the results expected of you, you must learn about the business. Your team is entrusting you to help grow their brand, develop positive media relationships, and even assist during a crisis if necessary.

When I first started as an assistant, there were many things I didn't know. Typically, when you join a company, you receive training on their systems and other aspects of the job. Of course, when applying for a position, you should already possess some knowledge about the job or the industry. However, being an assistant is different. An experienced assistant can work in any industry, but to truly excel, it's necessary to know the business.

Being an administrative professional goes far beyond typing documents, answering phones, or filing paperwork. It's so much bigger than that.

When I began my career, I didn't fully grasp the mission of the industry I was working in. My focus was simply on completing my tasks. For years, I worked with this mindset, and although I received promotions and awards, I wasn't seeing the bigger picture. That changed when a new director took over. She shook things up and focused on career development for the admin team. She helped us prepare for the next level. I know you might be thinking, "Next level as an admin? What does that mean?" Well, for many admins who had been with the company for years, the key to promotion was gaining technical expertise and a deeper understanding of the business line they supported.

At the time, I didn't see the value in learning about the business because I thought, "That's not my job." But once I did, my career really took off. I tapped into my creative side and became more helpful to my team by taking on responsibilities beyond basic admin tasks. I even led a project that brought my colleagues together to implement a process that streamlined our work. Knowing the business made me more than just an admin—I became a partner in the industry. And my employer recognized and rewarded me for going above and beyond. In fact, many of the admins I knew were able to move up to other roles because of this approach.

Know What Your Boss or Team Does

Your boss will be impressed if you demonstrate that you understand their business mission and values and have done your research. This shows that you care and have their best interests in mind. If you show no interest and aren't prepared, or if your work falls short of expectations, it sends the message that you aren't fully invested in supporting them. Regardless of the industry or company you work for, you must prove that you can offer undivided attention and bring fresh ideas to the table. This will help you stay ahead of the game, equipped with the knowledge to anticipate what's coming.

Great administrative professionals deeply understand their company's services, capabilities, and how those services benefit clients. This knowledge is crucial when presenting ideas and solutions. Top admin assistants also understand how their company stacks up against competitors, knowing both the strengths and weaknesses in the market. Great assistants spend time studying their company, the business, and the competitive landscape.

What Happens When an Admin Doesn't Know the Business?

Unfortunately, it's common for administrative professionals not to have a deep understanding of the business or how the company competes. This often leads to struggles with productivity. Admins may end up supporting clients that the business can't properly serve or fail to answer questions in a way that helps move projects forward. In short, they miss opportunities they could have otherwise capitalized on.

To succeed as an administrative professional, you must not only have a strong grasp of your own business but also understand the customer's business. To create value, admin assistants must know how their clients compete in their markets and the challenges and opportunities they face. This knowledge allows admin professionals to better position their company's services to help clients succeed. This deep understanding is a tremendous competitive advantage for any administrative professional.

Becoming an Expert in Your Role

The best administrative assistants use their knowledge and expertise to continuously educate themselves about their industry and their clients' businesses. They use this knowledge to create value, not just for their company but for the industry as a whole. When you become an expert in your field, the rewards are endless.

In government roles, administrative assistants may face a cap on promotions based on grade levels, meaning there's a limit to how high you can climb within that structure. In those situations, you might consider roles like becoming a supervisor or manager, where you can mentor and train others. That was the path I took. I stayed in the career I loved, but I also moved into a leadership role where I could share my years of experience with others.

If your current organization doesn't offer a clear path for advancement, consider finding a company that allows for growth and doesn't limit your potential.

Teekwa's Appraisal

"Teekwa demonstrates strong expertise in her role. She shows advanced knowledge of business processes within [company name] and a solid understanding of the industry as a whole. She maintains a high level of

knowledge regarding job content, policies, procedures, and the overall business landscape. Teekwa enjoys becoming a subject matter expert, as evidenced by her ability to improve business processes.

Your ability to see the big picture when it comes to office and data management requirements is outstanding. You have continuously improved processes with ease, and I look forward to hearing more of your innovative ideas and suggestions."

Chapter 7: Branding Yourself

In the workplace, your personal brand speaks before you even say a word. As an assistant, you're often the first point of contact, the frontline of the business. Your appearance is part of how you brand yourself, and it plays a huge role in how you're perceived. The way you present yourself physically communicates a message to others, whether you realize it or not. When you take pride in how you look, you're telling your boss, colleagues, and clients that you take your role seriously.

Your brand isn't just about skills and abilities—it's about how you carry yourself every day. While you may not think your physical appearance is important, it absolutely affects how others see you. Even if your boss doesn't consciously acknowledge it, dressing inappropriately or too casually can send the wrong message. In some cases, it can even hurt your chances for advancement. Simply put, people are more likely to trust and promote someone who looks the part.

Dressing the Part of Your Profession

No matter the industry or job title, every professional should have a personal brand that includes how they dress. For assistants, your attire becomes part of your brand, and it should align with both your role and the company's culture. Many companies have dress codes—usually business casual—but there is often room to personalize your look while still being professional. Your brand should align with the company's values, but still reflect who you are. If I had my way, I'd wear jeans and sneakers every day (LOL). But we must dress for success, especially if we're representing a business.

Even virtual assistants have to think about their personal brand, especially when meeting clients online via Zoom or Google Meet. While you might be working from home, your professionalism should still come across in how you present yourself on camera. You can get away with pajama bottoms (I know I do sometimes!), but from the waist up, make sure you're camera-ready in business attire.

A Case for Dressing Professionally

In one of my former workplaces, there was an assistant who was talented and friendly but often wore outfits that didn't align with professional expectations. Eventually, a client brought it to her attention, and she made changes. After that, more opportunities started opening up for her, and she ended up moving into the career she always wanted after receiving her master's degree. It's a great example of how something that seems small can have a huge impact on your career.

The Impact of Workplace Environment

Your workplace environment will influence how you dress. For example, in my previous role, unless we were working directly with high-level executives, business casual was the norm. However, when we had events or meetings with external clients, we were expected to wear business suits. Understanding your environment and dressing accordingly is key to establishing your brand in the workplace.

As workplaces shift to more casual dress codes, it's important to balance comfort with professionalism. Here are some rules to follow to ensure your appearance aligns with your personal brand and career goals:

12 Rules for Professional Branding Through Appearance:

1. **Know What's Appropriate for Your Industry**
   Every industry has different standards for dress. Familiarize yourself with these expectations and follow them closely.

2. **Wear Clothes That Fit**
   Ill-fitting clothes don't give off a polished, professional look. Make sure your clothes fit properly, from your outfit to your shoes and accessories.

3. Avoid Club or Party Attire

For women, choose power suits, blouses, and slacks that make you feel confident. For men, a well-tailored suit with a touch of personality, like stylish socks, can make a strong impression.

4. Wear Glasses That Fit

If you wear glasses, make sure they fit well and aren't constantly slipping down your nose. You don't want to be fidgeting with them during meetings.

5. Dry Your Hair

Never leave the house with wet hair. It can give the impression that you're disorganized, which could reflect poorly on your work.

6. Keep Your Purse or Briefcase Clean

Your personal items should be well-organized. A cluttered purse or briefcase can give the impression that you're disorganized.

7. Don't Wear Strong Perfume

Strong scents can be distracting and unpleasant for others. Stick with subtle fragrances or none at all.

8. Avoid Ankle Socks with Slacks

When you sit and cross your legs, no skin should show between your pants and your socks. It's a small detail that can make a big difference.

9. Don't Over-Accessorize

Accessories should complement your outfit, not overpower it. Noisy or excessive jewelry can be distracting.

10. Facial Hair Should Be Well-Groomed

For men, make sure your facial hair is neatly trimmed and doesn't overwhelm your face. Choose a style that suits your features.

11. **Wear Colors That Convey Authority**

    Darker colors like navy, black, and deep gray often convey more authority and professionalism than lighter shades. Choose your colors carefully, especially if you're giving a presentation.

12. **Avoid Neon and Flashy Clothing**

    Both men and women should be cautious about bright, flashy colors. They can be visually distracting and take attention away from your message.

Chapter 8: Professional Development

Just like in any other profession, assistants must stay current with their skills and be aware of daily changes in their industry. I firmly believe that you don't need a college degree to be a professional assistant. However, many companies now require at least a bachelor's degree. When I began my career as an assistant, I didn't have a degree, but I worked as if I did. If this is your chosen field, don't let the lack of a degree stop you from pursuing your dream. There's always someone willing to take a chance on you, just as they did for me. However, it's essential to take professional learning courses to improve your knowledge, competency, and effectiveness. I'm here to help you reach that next level.

For seasoned assistants, professional development should always be a priority. By taking online training, attending conferences, and participating in seminars, you can sharpen the skills where you may need improvement. I can help you find a mentor, join my community, which provide invaluable support.

My group will discusses challenges, offers guidance, builds, confidence, and focuses on strategies to ensure you continue to add value to your career.

Start your journey by joining my Community, VAAEN.ORG

Should Administrative Professionals Pursue More Education?

Whether you're seeking a college degree, taking continuing education classes, attending a one-day workshop, getting a certification, or reading self-study materials like The Effective Admin, it's all beneficial. While pursuing additional education isn't always necessary for every admin job or career, it can certainly be helpful.

I view all learning methods as valuable. I've known people with college degrees who are less productive or successful than those who are self-taught, and vice versa. It goes both ways. Each person is different in their work ethic and ambition—those traits can't be taught. What education and continuous learning offer access to new ideas, information, and knowledge. It's up to you to learn, retain, and apply what's offered.

Most importantly, it's up to YOU to decide how you'll use that knowledge. You must transfer what you've learned into your administrative role and implement it in your workplace.

You can gain knowledge, ideas, and information from various sources. I favor all learning methods, not just formal higher education. Learning helps you find or create new processes to improve current procedures in your job. Educational resources can spark creativity, and you don't have to be born creative to excel. Sometimes, it takes exposure to new ideas to inspire creativity. A book might present a concept (let's call it "X"), and you might realize that making one small change to "X" could improve how "Y" is done in your office. Does it make the process quicker or reduce errors? Often, you need that outside element to spark innovation.

Career administrative professionals want to stay motivated and enthusiastic about their jobs, even after 10, 20, or 30+ years on the job. One way to maintain that excitement is by learning new skills and ideas and applying them to new areas of your job. Let your manager know, "I just learned about X, so I can help you with Y now." Watch their eyes light up when they hear you took the initiative to continue learning in your field.

Learning opportunities also allow you to see how other administrative professionals are doing things today. You might think, "I've been doing this the best way for years," or you may find yourself saying, "Oh, what a great way to do that task—I never thought of doing it that way."

Even if you feel like you know everything you need to know for your job, educational materials can be great for refreshing your memory. After all, many of us forget where we put our keys, so how can we be expected to remember every detail of every skill or task in the office?

These are just some of the reasons why I advocate for continuing education, whether through reading trade magazines, self-study tip sheets like The Effective Admin, or attending in-person or online classes. Choose something to refresh your skills year-round, every year.

Chapter 9: Following Up

Following up is an essential skill that you need to practice daily. It's a common mistake for assistants to avoid follow-up, often out of fear of being annoying or bothersome. This can happen especially when trying to set up meetings or retrieve signed paperwork from a coach or speaker. Let's be real—if I have a task that requires assistance from someone else, I'll do whatever is necessary to get what I need, even if that means involving someone with authority. I have no problem making that call to get things done, as long as I handle everything professionally.

It can be frustrating when you have a full plate of tasks and completing them depends on someone else. But follow-up is a crucial part of your job. Don't shy away from it. Be prepared, have your ducks in a row, and keep moving forward. This is part of your responsibility, whether you like it or not.

I remember working in a role where letters had to be processed daily. The admin wasn't responsible for the letter's content, but we were the gatekeepers. We ensured the letters were on the correct template, with the fields properly formatted and the necessary signatures obtained before they went out. Deadlines were crucial. If a team member sent the wrong template, it was our responsibility to correct it. We had some outliers who continued sending the wrong templates, which slowed down our process.

One individual frustrated me because they repeatedly made the same mistake. I found myself following up with them daily, even going to their cubicle to nudge them to send the corrected letter. Let me offer a tip: Don't copy and paste into a template—it will mess up the formatting, creating more work for someone else to fix. After a few frustrating incidents, I had to involve management to get the job done. Let's just say, after that, I never had the problem again!

How Can I Help You?

Through my training, I can help you develop follow-up techniques using scenarios, role-playing, and tips tailored to various situations.

Here are a few tips to get started:

1. **Be Persistent and Consistent**
   Once a request has been made, give at least a week before following up, depending on the nature of the request. Don't be overbearing by sending daily emails. If you haven't received a response after two follow-ups, make a phone call.

2. **Switch It Up**
   If you're not getting any response, try changing your approach. Instead of sending the same email at the same time and day, alter the subject line, or send the email at a different time. Consider that mornings might be too busy for the recipient.

3. **Be Polite**
   Stay professional, even if you're frustrated. Take a deep breath before sending your email or making a call. If necessary, ask a colleague to review your email to ensure it sounds polite.

4. **Never Stop Trying**
   Think outside the box when following up. Adapt your methods as needed to get the response you need.

Chapter 10: Balance in the Workplace

Maintaining balance at work is crucial for managing stress. If you're feeling overwhelmed, talk to your manager about reevaluating your job responsibilities. Every company promotes balance to some extent, but it's up to you to find and maintain that balance for yourself.

Over the years, I always sought ways to improve my skills and take on more projects. While I was honored to be asked to lead projects, it sometimes became overwhelming. I found myself taking work home, which took time away from my family. Learning to say "no" doesn't mean you're incapable—it means you recognize your limits and want to maintain the quality of your work.

Saying "no" can prevent mediocre results. When I take on a project, I want to deliver my best work. Communicating with your manager about your workload helps balance responsibilities within the department.

If you work with me, I'll guide you through strategies for maintaining balance at work, ensuring you remain productive without sacrificing your well-being.

Workplace Etiquette

Respect Your Colleagues

As a professional assistant, you must be friendly, approachable, and willing to assist everyone, including fellow assistants. Learn your coworkers' names and greet them warmly. This helps build respect, trust, and a collaborative work environment.

Be Reliable

Being reliable is one of the most valued qualities in an assistant. Reliability can take many forms, from punctuality to communication. Proactively respond to emails and inquiries within 24 to 48 hours, and always keep people informed of the status of their requests.

Start and Finish Strong

Deliver high-quality work by starting strong and following through. Managing your commitments and prioritizing tasks is crucial to being an effective assistant.

Bonus: Embracing AI as an Administrative Professional

Let's talk about AI and why administrative professionals shouldn't fear it. Yes, technology is advancing at an incredible pace but let me assure you that AI is not new—it's been around for decades. AI has been shaping the way businesses operate for years. What's changing now is that it's becoming more visible in roles like ours, leading some to feel uneasy about its potential impact on their jobs.

I get it; new technology can feel intimidating. Even my 13-year-old son is learning how to use AI, and I take every opportunity to teach him the positive aspects of technology. I challenge him to think about how he can use these tools to his advantage, how it can make his life easier, and how he can become marketable by learning how it all works. This generation is growing up immersed in technology in ways we never were, and I encourage him to embrace it as a powerful tool for future opportunities.

The same applies to us as administrative professionals. Instead of being afraid, we should ask ourselves: *How can AI help me do my job more efficiently? How can I use this technology to my advantage and enhance my skills?*

AI is not here to take our jobs; it's here to make them easier. Let's explore how:

1. **Streamlining Mundane Tasks:**
   AI can handle repetitive tasks, allowing you to focus on more meaningful work. For example, instead of manually scheduling appointments or organizing meeting times, AI tools can analyze calendars and find the best time slots for everyone. Tools like **x.ai** and **Calendly** automate meeting scheduling by cross-referencing availability across multiple participants.

2. **Taking Meeting Minutes:**
   Who still takes meeting minutes manually anymore? While it's true that some organizations may require human note-takers due to security purposes, many professionals now rely on AI

tools to handle this task. AI-powered platforms like **Otter.ai** can record meetings, transcribe them, and automatically generate summaries, action items, and key takeaways—saving you time and effort while ensuring accuracy.

3. **Data Management and Extraction:**
As administrative professionals, we deal with a lot of data—whether it's pulling information from documents, emails, or images. AI can extract this information and turn it into usable data, streamlining tasks like report generation, data entry, or organizing key details. Tools like **DocuSign** or **Adobe Sensei** can quickly extract and manage data from scanned documents, which makes our job much easier.

4. **Report Generation and Analysis:**
Let's say you're responsible for creating reports based on large sets of data. AI can assist by analyzing the data and generating insights. Tools like **Tableau** and **Power BI**, for example, use AI-driven analytics to pull out trends, patterns, and actionable insights, providing support for better decision-making.

5. **Sending Reminders and Managing Tasks:**
AI can help manage deadlines, tasks, and reminders by automating notifications. This feature is particularly useful for administrative assistants juggling multiple projects and team members. For instance, tools like **Trello** or **ClickUp** integrate AI to keep you on top of your projects, sending timely reminders or flagging overdue tasks.

6. **Enhanced Communication with Chatbots:**
AI-powered chatbots are becoming increasingly common in business settings. They can be used to answer routine queries from clients, manage customer service tasks, or even assist team members with frequently asked questions. This allows you to focus on more complex inquiries and reduces the amount of time spent on repetitive communication tasks.

7. **Translation Services:**

If your company operates globally or works with international clients, AI tools like **Google Translate** or **DeepL** can quickly translate documents and emails in various languages, ensuring effective communication across borders.

Sample AI Prompt for Administrative Assistants

If you're new to AI, why not create a free ChatGPT account? Familiarize yourself with how AI can streamline your daily tasks. Here's a sample prompt to help you get started with ChatGPT:

Sample Prompt: *"I'm an administrative assistant managing a busy executive's calendar. Please help me draft a polite email reminder for a meeting, summarize the key points from a 30-minute meeting recording, and suggest the best way to organize our shared team folder for optimal efficiency."*

This prompt can help you with the following:

- Writing professional emails   quickly.
- Summarizing meetings so you   don't have to sift through notes manually.
- Offering suggestions for   organizations to keep their workspaces efficient.

AI is your partner, not your competition! Take the leap, explore AI tools like ChatGPT, and see how they can make your workday more productive and manageable.

The key takeaway here is that AI is an **enhancer**, not a replacement. It's designed to take over the mundane, time-consuming tasks so that we, as administrative professionals, can focus on more strategic and impactful work. AI can't replicate the human touch—the empathy, creativity, and decision-making that we bring to the table. Instead, it empowers us to be more efficient, accurate, and valuable to the teams we support.

Think about it: How much more effective could you be if you had AI tools assisting you in your day-to-day tasks? Could you focus more on problem-solving, improving processes, or supporting your team in ways that require your unique skills and insights?

Like I tell my son, new technology is a tool, and we should learn how to use it to our advantage. So, instead of worrying about AI replacing our jobs, let's learn how to integrate it into our work, embrace it, and use it to enhance our productivity and job satisfaction. AI is here to stay, and those who master it will be positioned for long-term success in their careers.

Here are some great resources:

- How to Win Friends and Influence People" by Dale Carnegie
- The 7 Habits of Highly Effective People" by Stephen R. Covey
- Quiet: The Power of Introverts in a World That Can't Stop Talking" by Susan Cain
- Sign up for a FREE ChatGPT account - chapgpt.com

Are you ready to elevate your skills and push yourself to the next level? Let's work together to achieve tangible results and excel in your role as an administrative professional!

Email your inquiries: Info@teekwascarborough.com

Website:

Vaaen.org

Teekwa.com

ON SOCIAL MEDIA

Follow us on Instagram @VAAENETWORK @COACHTEEKWA

www.ingramcontent.com/pod-product-compliance
Lightning Source LLC
Chambersburg PA
CBHW052123030426
42335CB00025B/3087